TOTALLY BLACKED OUT™

Classic Lit...
BLACKOUT GAMES™

▲adamsmedia
Avon, Massachusetts

Published by
Adams Media, a division of F+W Media, Inc.
57 Littlefield Street, Avon, MA 02322. U.S.A.
www.adamsmedia.com

Totally Blacked Out and Blackout Games are trademarks of
Adams Media, a division of F+W Media, Inc.

ISBN-10: 1-4405-3259-1
ISBN-13: 978-1-4405-3259-7

Printed in the United States of America.

10   9   8   7   6   5   4   3   2   1

This publication is designed to provide accurate and authoritative information
with regard to the subject matter covered. It is sold with the understanding
that the publisher is not engaged in rendering legal, accounting, or other
professional advice. If legal advice or other expert assistance is required, the
services of a competent professional person should be sought.

　　—From a *Declaration of Principles* jointly adopted by a Committee of the
American Bar Association and a Committee of Publishers and Associations

Many of the designations used by manufacturers and sellers to distinguish
their product are claimed as trademarks. Where those designations appear in
this book and Adams Media was aware of a trademark claim, the designations
have been printed with initial capital letters.

This book is available at quantity discounts for bulk purchases.
For information, please call 1-800-289-0963.

Contents

Introduction

Finally—a word game that *encourages* you to scribble outside the lines! Combining the simplicity of word search with the creativity of magnetic poetry, *Classic Lit Blackout Games*™ blows those boring, been-there-done-that puzzles out of the water.

Taking gaming to next level, this book inspires you to think outside the puzzle and look at your favorite (or least favorite) authors' works with a new perspective. Through blacking out words and phrases, you can transform classic pieces of literature into outrageous, poetic, or truly bizarre messages. You'll feel like a kid again as you black out words in the shape of a skull in a passage from *Hamlet* or create a fortune cookie message with words plucked ~~struck~~ from *The Canterbury Tales*. With *Classic Lit Blackout Games*™, you'll absolutely love reinventing the words of Austen, Dickens, Hawthorne, and more—one blacked-out word at a time!

HOW TO USE THIS BOOK

Inside this book, you'll find more than 100 puzzles to complete. Each chapter includes detailed directions and a completed example to inspire you. You'll create original messages by blacking out unused words with a marker, but be careful—once they're hidden behind that layer of ink, they're gone forever!

Here's how you get started:

1. Grab a marker or pen; the darker the better.
2. Read the passage carefully and think about what messages can be created out of your favorite words.
3. Make a small mark identifying each word you want to use in your poem (unless you have an awesome memory).
4. ~~Cross~~ black out everything else.
5. When you're done, your message will read like a complete (and perhaps incredibly poetic!) thought.

NOTE:

To prevent your genius from bleeding through the pages, please place a piece of paper or card stock behind the page before you begin your Totally Blacked Out™ fun.

CHAPTER ONE

Literature's Alphabet

We're starting with the basics for this first chapter: the alphabet. Sure, it sounds like a breeze, but you've really never seen the alphabet quite like this before. In the following puzzles, you'll have to create a message only using words that begin with the letters assigned to that puzzle, so make sure to pay close attention to what your favorite authors have written. If you get stuck, find some inspiration in the sample puzzle below. You may also find it helpful to also search *within* words to help complete your message. As you can see from the example, you don't always have to use the words in the order they appear.

Create a message using words that begin with the letter "D."

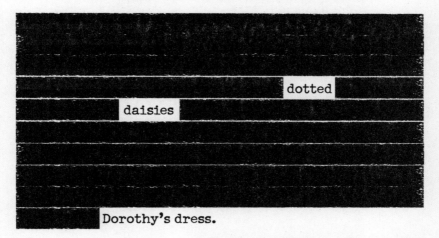

From Frank L. Baum's *The Wonderful Wizard of Oz*

Message: daisies dotted Dorothy's dress.

1

At the termination of this sentence I started and, for a moment, paused; for it appeared to me (although I at once concluded that my excited fancy had deceived me)—it appeared to me that, from some very remote portion of the mansion, there came, indistinctly to my ears, what might have been, in its exact similarity of character, the echo (but a stifled and dull one certainly) of the very cracking and ripping sound which Sir Launcelot had so particularly described. It was, beyond doubt, the coincidence alone which had arrested my attention; for, amid the rattling of the sashes of the casements, and the ordinary commingled noises of the still increasing storm, the sound, in itself, had nothing, surely, which should have interested or disturbed me.

From Edgar Allan Poe's *The Fall of the House of Usher*

Create a message using words that begin with consonants.

In the garden of the Tuileries he had lingered, on two or three spots, to look; it was as if the wonderful Paris spring had stayed him as he roamed. The prompt Paris morning struck its cheerful notes—in a soft breeze and a sprinkled smell, in the light flit, over the garden-floor, of bareheaded girls with the buckled strap of oblong boxes, in the type of ancient thrifty persons basking betimes where terrace-walls were warm, in the blue-frocked brass-labelled officialism of humble rakers and scrapers, in the deep references of a straight-pacing priest or the sharp ones of a white-gaitered red-legged soldier. He watched little brisk figures, figures whose movement was as the tick of the great Paris clock.

From Henry James's *The Ambassadors*

5

Create a message using words that begin with consonants.

We have the same swamps and mosquitoes; the same disease and want; the typhoid, the diphtheria, the burning villages. We are confronted by the degradation of our country, brought on by the fierce struggle for existence of the human race. It is the consequence of the ignorance and unconsciousness of starving, shivering, sick humanity that, to save its children, instinctively snatches at everything that can warm it and still its hunger. So it destroys everything it can lay its hands on, without a thought for the morrow. And almost everything has gone, and nothing has been created to take its place. (Coldly) But I see by your face that I am not interesting you.

From Anton Pavlovich Chekhov's *Uncle Vanya*

Create a message using words that begin with vowels.

His dull expectation of the usual disagreeable routine with an aged patient... added to his general disbelief in Middlemarch charms, made a doubly effective background to this vision of Rosamond, whom old Featherstone made haste ostentatiously to introduce as his niece, though he had never thought it worth while to speak of Mary Garth in that light. Nothing escaped Lydgate in Rosamond's graceful behavior: how delicately she waived the notice which the old man's want of taste had thrust upon her by a quiet gravity, not showing her dimples on the wrong occasion, but showing them afterwards in speaking to Mary, to whom she addressed herself with so much good-natured interest, that Lydgate, after quickly examining Mary more fully than he had done before, saw an adorable kindness in Rosamond's eyes.

From George Eliot's *Middlemarch*

Create a message using words that begin with the letters "C," "D," "E," and "F."

When he was present she had no eyes for any one else. Every thing he did, was right. Every thing he said, was clever. If their evenings at the park were concluded with cards, he cheated himself and all the rest of the party to get her a good hand. If dancing formed the amusement of the night, they were partners for half the time; and when obliged to separate for a couple of dances, were careful to stand together and scarcely spoke a word to any body else. Such conduct made them of course most exceedingly laughed at; but ridicule could not shame, and seemed hardly to provoke them.

From Jane Austen's *Sense and Sensibility*

Create a message using words that begin with consonants.

We look before and after,
And pine for what is not;
Our sincerest laughter
With some pain is fraught;
Our sweetest songs are those that tell of saddest
    thought.
Yet, if we could scorn
Hate and pride and fear,
If we were things born
Not to shed a tear,
I know not how thy joy we ever should come near.
Better than all measures
Of delightful sound,
Better than all treasures
That in books are found,
Thy skill to poet were, thou scorner of the
    ground!
Teach me half the gladness
That thy brain must know,
Such harmonious madness
From my lips would flow
The world should listen then as I am listening
    now.

From Percy Bysshe Shelley's "To a Skylark"

13

Create a message using words that begin with the letters "F," "G," "H," and "I."

What we call real estate—the solid ground to build a house on—is the broad foundation on which nearly all the guilt of this world rests. A man will commit almost any wrong,— he will heap up an immense pile of wickedness, as hard as granite, and which will weigh as heavily upon his soul, to eternal ages,—only to build a great, gloomy, dark-chambered mansion, for himself to die in, and for his posterity to be miserable in. He lays his own dead corpse beneath the underpinning, as one may say, and hangs his frowning picture on the wall, and, after thus converting himself into an evil destiny, expects his remotest great-grandchildren to be happy there.

From Nathaniel Hawthorne's *The House of Seven Gables*

CHAPTER TWO

Few and Far Between

Let's find out how much you really love your favorite authors. To solve the puzzles in this chapter, you'll need to black out the least amount of words possible. With several world-renowned passages in front of you, it may not seem like a hard task to create your very own poem, but the difficulty here lies in creating an *original* message that sounds more like you than straight from the mouths of these famous writers. When you're feeling a little creative, take a look at the example we've done and get ready to pen your very own masterpiece.

now, in broad daylight, she looked   ,
with

long lashes   ,
relieved

her hair, of a very dark brown, was clustered

, according to the fashion of those times

her dress, also in the mode of the day, was of
purple cloth,   of Spanish trim

;   not so common
then as now

From Charlotte Brontë's *Jane Eyre*

Message: now, in broad daylight, she looked, with long lashes, relieved/ her hair, of a very dark brown, was clustered, according to the fashion of those times/ her dress, also in the mode of the day, was of purple cloth, of Spanish trim; not so common then as now

The raven himself is hoarse

That croaks the fatal entrance of Duncan

Under my battlements. Come, you spirits

That tend on mortal thoughts, unsex me here

And fill me from the crown to the toe top-
full

Of direst cruelty! Make thick my blood,

Stop up the access and passage to remorse,

That no compunctious visitings of nature

Shake my fell purpose nor keep peace between

The effect and it! Come to my woman's breasts,

And take my milk for gall, you murdering
ministers,

Wherever in your sightless substances

You wait on nature's mischief! Come, thick
night,

And pall thee in the dunnest smoke of hell

That my keen knife see not the wound it makes

Nor heaven peep through the blanket of the
dark

To cry, "Hold, hold!"

From William Shakespeare's *The Tragedie of Macbeth*

I smiled to myself at the sight of this money: "O drug!" said I, aloud, "what art thou good for? Thou art not worth to me—no, not the taking off the ground; one of those knives is worth all this heap; I have no manner of use for thee—e'en remain where thou art, and go to the bottom as a creature whose life is not worth saving." However, upon second thoughts I took it away; and wrapping all this in a piece of canvas, I began to think of making another raft; but while I was preparing this, I found the sky overcast, and the wind began to rise, and in a quarter of an hour it blew a fresh gale from the shore.

From Daniel Defoe's *The Life and Adventures of Robinson Crusoe*

About two years before the time of which I am now writing, and about a year and a half before the time of his death, the Colonel came unexpectedly to my lady's house in London. It was the night of Miss Rachel's birthday, the twenty-first of June; and there was a party in honour of it, as usual. I received a message from the footman to say that a gentleman wanted to see me. Going up into the hall, there I found the Colonel, wasted, and worn, and old, and shabby, and as wild and as wicked as ever.

From Wilkie Collins's *The Moonstone*

Beowulf donned then his battle-equipments,

Cared little for life; inlaid and most ample,

The hand-woven corslet which could cover his
    body,

Must the wave-deeps explore, that war might
    be powerless

To harm the great hero, and the hating one's
    grasp might

Not peril his safety; his head was protected

By the light-flashing helmet that should mix
    with the bottoms,

Trying the eddies, treasure-emblazoned,

Encircled with jewels, as in seasons long past

The weapon-smith worked it, wondrously made
    it,

With swine-bodies fashioned it, that
    thenceforward no longer

Brand might bite it, and battle-sword hurt it.

And that was not least of helpers in prowess

He has Unferth's sword in his hand.

That Hrothgar's spokesman had lent him when
    straitened

From *Beowulf*

This man, whose costume was concealed by the crowd which surrounded him, did not appear to be more than five and thirty years of age; nevertheless, he was bald; he had merely a few tufts of thin, gray hair on his temples; his broad, high forehead had begun to be furrowed with wrinkles, but his deep-set eyes sparkled with extraordinary youthfulness, an ardent life, a profound passion. He kept them fixed incessantly on the gypsy, and, while the giddy young girl of sixteen danced and whirled, for the pleasure of all, his revery seemed to become more and more sombre.

From Victor Hugo's *The Hunchback of Notre-Dame*

They were not born today nor yesterday;

They die not; and none knoweth whence they
   sprang.

I was not like, who feared no mortal's frown,

To disobey these laws and so provoke

The wrath of Heaven. I knew that I must die,

E'en hadst thou not proclaimed it; and if
   death

Is thereby hastened, I shall count it gain.

For death is gain to him whose life, like mine,

Is full of misery. Thus my lot appears

Not sad, but blissful; for had I endured

To leave my mother's son unburied there,

I should have grieved with reason, but not
   now.

And if in this thou judgest me a fool,

Methinks the judge of folly's not acquit.

From Sophocles's *Antigone*

29

It was the best of times, it was the worst of times, it was the age of wisdom, it was the age of foolishness, it was the epoch of belief, it was the epoch of incredulity, it was the season of Light, it was the season of Darkness, it was the spring of hope, it was the winter of despair, we had everything before us, we had nothing before us, we were all going direct to Heaven, we were all going direct the other way—in short, the period was so far like the present period, that some of its noisiest authorities insisted on its being received, for good or for evil, in the superlative degree of comparison only.

From Charles Dickens's *A Tale of Two Cities*

To Sherlock Holmes she is always *the* woman. I have seldom heard him mention her under any other name. In his eyes she eclipses and predominates the whole of her sex. It was not that he felt any emotion akin to love for Irene Adler. All emotions, and that one particularly, were abhorrent to his cold, precise but admirably balanced mind. He was, I take it, the most perfect reasoning and observing machine that the world has seen, but as a lover he would have placed himself in a false position. He never spoke of the softer passions, save with a gibe and a sneer. They were admirable things for the observer—excellent for drawing the veil from men's motives and actions.

From Sir Arthur Conan Doyle's *Adventures of Sherlock Holmes*

CHAPTER THREE

The Greatest Expectation

Time for a ~~little~~ lot of fun! In this chapter, we're giving you full permission to wreak havoc on all your favorite (or most loathed) stories. That's right, in order to finish the following puzzles, you'll need to create a message by blacking out as many words as possible. Just remember that you should still be left with a complete thought at the end of each ink-filled puzzle. If you're looking for more of a challenge, try to beat our sample puzzle or test your blackout skills against your friends.

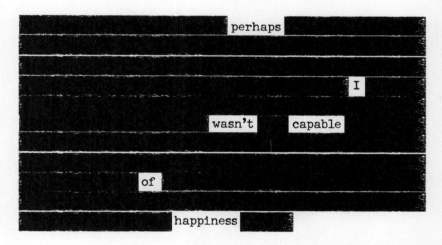

From Fyodor Dostoyevsky's *Crime and Punishment*

Message: perhaps I wasn't capable of happiness

If you don't make it up with him now, I really shall think you are very wicked. I am becoming like Lady Midlothian;—I can't understand it. I know you want to be his wife, and I know he wants to be your husband, and the only thing that keeps you apart is your obstinacy,—just because you have said you wouldn't have him. My belief is that if Lady Midlothian and the rest of us were to pat you on the back, and tell you how right you were, you'd ask him to take you, out of defiance. You may be sure of this, Alice; if you refuse him now, it'll be for the last time.

From Anthony Trollope's *Can You Forgive Her?*

They went eagerly to the battle, and gave many great strokes. Sir Accolon had all advantage on his side, for he had the real Excalibur, Morgan le Fay having so ordained that King Arthur should have been slain that day. King Arthur's sword never bit like Sir Accolon's, and almost every stroke Sir Accolon gave wounded sore, so that it was a marvel that Arthur stood. Almost from the first it seemed to him that the sword in Accolon's hand must be Excalibur, but he was so full of knighthood that knightly he endured the pain of the many wounds, and held out as well as he might until his sword brake at the cross and fell in the grass among the blood.

From Sir Thomas Malory's *Stories of King Arthur and His Knights*

The brown current ran swiftly out of the heart of darkness, bearing us down towards the sea with twice the speed of our upward progress; and Kurtz's life was running swiftly too, ebbing, ebbing out of his heart into the sea of inexorable time. The manager was very placid, he had no vital anxieties now, he took us both in with a comprehensive and satisfied glance: the 'affair' had come off as well as could be wished. I saw the time approaching when I would be left alone of the party of 'unsound method.' The pilgrims looked upon me with disfavor. I was, so to speak, numbered with the dead. It is strange how I accepted this unforeseen partnership, this choice of nightmares forced upon me in the tenebrous land invaded by these mean and greedy phantoms.

From Joseph Conrad's *Heart of Darkness*

A moment before the ghost of the ancient kingdom of the Danes had looked forth through the vesture of the hazewrapped City. Now, at the name of the fabulous artificer, he seemed to hear the noise of dim waves and to see a winged form flying above the waves and slowly climbing the air. What did it mean? Was it a quaint device opening a page of some medieval book of prophecies and symbols, a hawk-like man flying sunward above the sea, a prophecy of the end he had been born to serve and had been following through the mists of childhood and boyhood, a symbol of the artist forging anew in his workshop out of the sluggish matter of the earth a new soaring impalpable imperishable being?

From James Joyce's *A Portrait of an Artist as a Young Man*

This was cold comfort. Somehow, without Tommy, all the savour went out of the adventure, and, for the first time, Tuppence felt doubtful of success. While they had been together she had never questioned it for a minute. Although she was accustomed to take the lead, and to pride herself on her quick-wittedness, in reality she had relied upon Tommy more than she realized at the time. There was something so eminently sober and clear-headed about him, his common sense and soundness of vision were so unvarying, that without him Tuppence felt much like a rudderless ship. It was curious that Julius, who was undoubtedly much cleverer than Tommy, did not give her the same feeling of support.

From Agatha Christie's *The Secret Adversary*

Restless Amata lay, her swelling breast
Fir'd with disdain for Turnus dispossess'd,
And the new nuptials of the Trojan guest.
From her black bloody locks the Fury shakes
Her darling plague, the fav'rite of her snakes;
With her full force she threw the poisonous
    dart,
And fix'd it deep within Amata's heart,
That, thus envenom'd, she might kindle rage,
And sacrifice to strife her house husband's
    age.
Unseen, unfelt, the fiery serpent skims
Betwixt her linen and her naked limbs;
His baleful breath inspiring, as he glides,
Now like a chain around her neck he rides,
Now like a fillet to her head repairs,
And with his circling volumes folds her hairs.
At first the silent venom slid with ease,
And seiz'd her cooler senses by degrees.

From Virgil's *Aeneid*

The memories of childhood and of Levin's friendship with her dead brother gave a special poetic charm to her relations with him. His love for her, of which she felt certain, was flattering and delightful to her; and it was pleasant for her to think of Levin. In her memories of Vronsky there always entered a certain element of awkwardness, though he was in the highest degree well-bred and at ease, as though there were some false note—not in Vronsky, he was very simple and nice, but in herself, while with Levin she felt perfectly simple and clear. But, on the other hand, directly she thought of the future with Vronsky, there arose before her a perspective of brilliant happiness; with Levin the future seemed misty.

From Leo Tolstoy's *Anna Karenin*

I was a-trembling, because I'd got to decide, forever, betwixt two things, and I knowed it. I studied a minute, sort of holding my breath, and then says to myself: "All right, then, I'll GO to hell"—and tore it up. It was awful thoughts and awful words, but they was said. And I let them stay said; and never thought no more about reforming. I shoved the whole thing out of my head, and said I would take up wickedness again, which was in my line, being brung up to it, and the other warn't. And for a starter I would go to work and steal Jim out of slavery again; and if I could think up anything worse, I would do that, too.

From Mark Twain's *The Adventures of Huckleberry Finn*

The White Whale swam before him as the monomaniac incarnation of all those malicious agencies which some deep men feel eating in them, till they are left living on with half a heart and half a lung. That intangible malignity which has been from the beginning; to whose dominion even the modern Christians ascribe one-half of the worlds; which the ancient Ophites of the east reverenced in their statue devil;—Ahab did not fall down and worship it like them; but deliriously transferring its idea to the abhorred white whale, he pitted himself, all mutilated, against it. All that most maddens and torments; all that stirs up the lees of things; all truth with malice in it; all that cracks the sinews and cakes the brain; all the subtle demonisms of life and thought; all evil, to crazy Ahab, were visibly personified, and made practically assailable in Moby Dick. He piled upon the whale's white hump the sum of all the general rage and hate felt by his whole race from Adam down; and then, as if his chest had been a mortar, he burst his hot heart's shell upon it.

From Herman Melville's *Moby-Dick: The Whale*

A Different Point of View

We're turning everything upside down with this chapter. Just like before, you'll need to black out words to create a message, but this time, you'll need to construct a sentence that can be read from the bottom to the top of the page. Still can't wrap your head around this new outlook? Use our blackout example below for ideas on how to start creating your message. You're sure to have a great time starting at the bottom with these topsy-turvy puzzles!

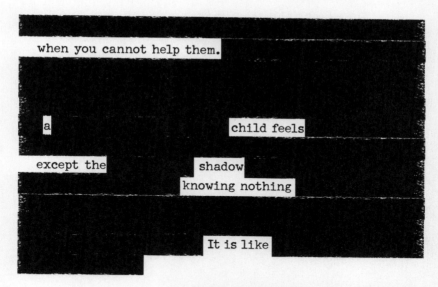

when you cannot help them.

a   child feels

except the   shadow
knowing nothing

It is like

From Anton Pavlovich Chekhov's *Uncle Vanya*

Message: It is like knowing nothing except the shadow a child feels when you cannot help them.

I never noticed it from here before.

I must be wonted to it—that's the reason.

The little graveyard where my people are!

So small the window frames the whole of it.

Not so much larger than a bedroom, is it?

There are three stones of slate and one of
　　marble,

Broad-shouldered little slabs there in the
　　sunlight

On the sidehill. We haven't to mind those.

But I understand: it is not the stones,

But the child's mound——"

"Don't, don't, don't, don't,:" she cried.

She withdrew shrinking from beneath his arm

That rested on the banister, and slid
　　downstairs;

And turned on him with such a daunting look

From Robert Frost's "Home Burial"

Well, she must talk about something. (He controls himself and sits down again). Oh, she'll be all right: don't you fuss. Pickering is in it with me. I've a sort of bet on that I'll pass her off as a duchess in six months. I started on her some months ago; and she's getting on like a house on fire. I shall win my bet. She has a quick ear; and she's been easier to teach than my middle-class pupils because she's had to learn a complete new language. She talks English almost as you talk French.

From George Bernard Shaw's *Pygmalion*

To be loved and chosen by a good man is the best and sweetest thing which can happen to a woman, and I sincerely hope my girls may know this beautiful experience... My dear girls, I am ambitious for you, but not to have you make a dash in the world, marry rich men merely because they are rich, or have splendid houses, which are not homes because love is wanting. Money is a needful and precious thing, and when well used, a noble thing, but I never want you to think it is the first or only prize to strive for. I'd rather see you poor men's wives, if you were happy, beloved, contented, than queens on thrones, without self-respect and peace.

From Louisa May Alcott's *Little Women*

Tho wrapping up her wrethed sterne arownd,

Lept fierce upon his shield, and her huge
traine

All suddenly about his body wound,

That hand or foot to stirre he strove in vaine:

God helpe the man so wrapt in Errours
endlesse traine.

His Lady sad to see his sore constraint,

Cride out, Now now Sir knight, shew what ye
bee,

Add faith unto your force, and be not faint:

Strangle her, else she sure will strangle thee.

That when he heard, in great perplexitie,

His gall did grate for griefe and high
disdaine,

And knitting all his force got one hand free,

Wherewith he grypt her gorge with so great
paine,

That soone to loose her wicked bands did her
constraine.

From Edmund Spenser's *The Faerie Queene*

She had done nothing to disturb their belief that she was awaiting his return in comfort, hoping against hope that his journey to Brazil would result in a short stay only, after which he would come to fetch her, or that he would write for her to join him; in any case that they would soon present a united front to their families and the world. This hope she still fostered. To let her parents know that she was a deserted wife, dependent, now that she had relieved their necessities, on her own hands for a living, after the *éclat* of a marriage which was to nullify the collapse of the first attempt, would be too much indeed.

From Thomas Hardy's *Tess of the d'Urbervilles*

Standardization is excellent, per se. When I buy an Ingersoll watch or a Ford, I get a better tool for less money, and I know precisely what I'm getting, and that leaves me more time and energy to be individual in. And—I remember once in London I saw a picture of an American suburb, in a toothpaste ad on the back of the Saturday Evening Post—an elm-lined snowy street of these new houses, Georgian some of 'em, or with low raking roofs and—The kind of street you'd find here in Zenith, say in Floral Heights. Open. Trees. Grass. And I was homesick! There's no other country in the world that has such pleasant houses. And I don't care if they ARE standardized. It's a corking standard!

From Sinclair Lewis's *Babbitt*

That sun, which erst with love my bosom
  warm'd

Had of fair truth unveil'd the sweet aspect,

By proof of right, and of the false reproof;

And I, to own myself convinc'd and free

Of doubt, as much as needed, rais'd my head

Erect for speech. But soon a sight appear'd,

Which, so intent to mark it, held me fix'd,

That of confession I no longer thought.

As through translucent and smooth glass, or
  wave

Clear and unmov'd, and flowing not so deep

As that its bed is dark, the shape returns

So faint of our impictur'd lineaments,

That on white forehead set a pearl as strong

Comes to the eye: such saw I many a face,

All stretch'd to speak, from whence I straight
  conceiv'd

Delusion opposite to that, which rais'd

Between the man and fountain, amorous flame.

From Dante Alighieri's *The Divine Comedy*

To say the truth, I had conceived a few scruples with relation to the distributive justice of princes upon those occasions. For instance, a crew of pirates are driven by a storm they know not whither; at length a boy discovers land from the topmast; they go on shore to rob and plunder, they see a harmless people, are entertained with kindness; they give the country a new name; they take formal possession of it for their king; they set up a rotten plank, or a stone, for a memorial; they murder two or three dozen of the natives, bring away a couple more, by force, for a sample; return home, and get their pardon. Here commences a new dominion acquired with a title by divine right.

From Jonathan Swift's *Gulliver's Travels into Several Remote Regions of the World*

CHAPTER FIVE

Switching Perspective

Think you've mastered flipping around messages? Think again. Like the previous chapter, you'll need to visualize the passages a little differently to solve the following puzzles. However, instead of creating a sentence that can be read from the bottom to the top of the page like before, this time you'll have to make it read from right to left. Not sure where to start? Glance at our sample for inspiration.

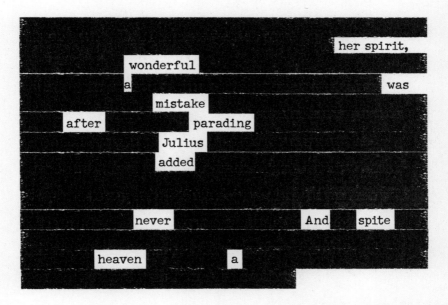

From Edith Wharton's The *House of Mirth*

Message: her spirit, wonderful was a mistake/ parading after Julius added spite and never a heaven

We are punished for our refusals. Every impulse that we strive to strangle broods in the mind and poisons us. The body sins once, and has done with its sin, for action is a mode of purification. Nothing remains then but the recollection of a pleasure, or the luxury of a regret. The only way to get rid of a temptation is to yield to it. Resist it, and your soul grows sick with longing for the things it has forbidden to itself, with desire for what its monstrous laws have made monstrous and unlawful. It has been said that the great events of the world take place in the brain. It is in the brain, and the brain only, that the great sins of the world take place also.

From Oscar Wilde's *The Picture of Dorian Gray*

What's done was well done. Thou canst never shake
  shake
My firm belief. A truce to argument.
For, had I sight, I know not with what eyes
I could have met my father in the shades,
Or my poor mother, since against the twain
I sinned, a sin no gallows could atone.
Aye, but, ye say, the sight of children joys
A parent's eyes. What, born as mine were born?
No, such a sight could never bring me joy;
Nor this fair city with its battlements,
Its temples and the statues of its gods,
Sights from which I, now wretchedst of all,
Once ranked the foremost Theban in all
  Thebes,
By my own sentence am cut off, condemned.

From Sophocles's *Oedipus the King*

Mrs. Morel, in her little rocking-chair that her husband had made for her when the first baby was coming, remained motionless, brooding. She was grieved, and bitterly sorry for the man who was hurt so much. But still, in her heart of hearts, where the love should have burned, there was a blank. Now, when all her woman's pity was roused to its full extent, when she would have slaved herself to death to nurse him and to save him, when she would have taken the pain herself, if she could, somewhere far away inside her, she felt indifferent to him and to his suffering. It hurt her most of all, this failure to love him, even when he roused her strong emotions. She brooded a while.

From D.H. Lawrence's *Sons and Lovers*

It is only now and then that there appears on the face of facts a sinister violence of intention—that indefinable something which forces it upon the mind and the heart of a man, that this complication of accidents or these elemental furies are coming at him with a purpose of malice, with a strength beyond control, with an unbridled cruelty that means to tear out of him his hope and his fear, the pain of his fatigue and his longing for rest: which means to smash, to destroy, to annihilate all he has seen, known, loved, enjoyed, or hated; all that is priceless and necessary— the sunshine, the memories, the future; which means to sweep the whole precious world utterly away from his sight by the simple and appalling act of taking his life.

From Joseph Conrad's *Lord Jim*

I too, as happens to every man once in his life, have been taken by Satan into the highest mountain in the earth, and when there he showed me all the kingdoms of the world, and as he said before, so said he to me, 'Child of earth, what wouldst thou have to make thee adore me?' I reflected long, for a gnawing ambition had long preyed upon me, and then I replied, 'Listen,—I have always heard of providence, and yet I have never seen him, or anything that resembles him, or which can make me believe that he exists. I wish to be providence myself, for I feel that the most beautiful, noblest, most sublime thing in the world, is to recompense and punish.

From Alexandre Dumas's *The Count of Monte Cristo*

I wish Jane success with all my heart; and if she were married to him to-morrow, I should think she had as good a chance of happiness as if she were to be studying his character for a twelvemonth. Happiness in marriage is entirely a matter of chance. If the dispositions of the parties are ever so well known to each other or ever so similar beforehand, it does not advance their felicity in the least. They always continue to grow sufficiently unlike afterwards to have their share of vexation; and it is better to know as little as possible of the defects of the person with whom you are to pass your life.

From Jane Austen's *Pride and Prejudice*

It is a chaos—a confused multitude, where everybody seeks pleasure and scarcely any one finds it, at least as it appeared to me. I made a short stay there. On my arrival I was robbed of all I had by pickpockets at the fair of St. Germain. I myself was taken for a robber and was imprisoned for eight days, after which I served as corrector of the press to gain the money necessary for my return to Holland on foot. I knew the whole scribbling rabble, the party rabble, the fanatic rabble. It is said that there are very polite people in that city, and I wish to believe it.

From Voltaire's *Candide*

We are apprehensive that, after all the labour which we should employ in painting this scene, the said reader would be very apt to skip it entirely over, we have saved ourselves that trouble. To say the truth, we have, from this reason alone, often done great violence to the luxuriance of our genius, and have left many excellent descriptions out of our work, which would otherwise have been in it. And this suspicion, to be honest, arises, as is generally the case, from our own wicked heart; for we have, ourselves, been very often most horridly given to jumping, as we have run through the pages of voluminous historians.

From Henry Fielding's *Tom Jones*

A Classic Q & A

In this chapter, you'll have to answer the fun (and often ridiculous) questions we've provided. Finding an answer in the puzzle may be a little tricky, so feel free to use a little imagination and a lot of creativity to uncover the possibilities for responses. As you can see from our blackout example, your message may not 100 percent truthful when all is said and done, but it's guaranteed be absolutely hilarious! Now, the real question is: Are you ready for this challenge?

Where is the best place to find a clue?

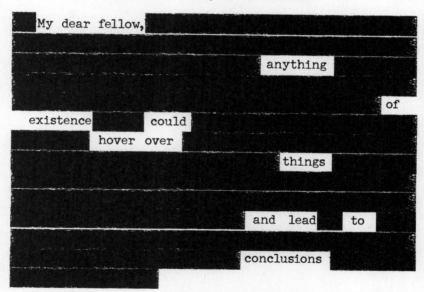

From Sir Arthur Conan Doyle's *Adventures of Sherlock Holmes*

Message: My dear fellow, anything of existence could hover over things and lead to conclusions

91

How do you make the best out of a bad situation?

He had pleased himself, many times during his illness, with thinking of all that Mr. Brownlow and Mrs. Bedwin would say to him: and what delight it would be to tell them how many long days and nights he had passed in reflecting on what they had done for him, and in bewailing his cruel separation from them. The hope of eventually clearing himself with them, too, and explaining how he had been forced away, had buoyed him up, and sustained him, under many of his recent trials; and now, the idea that they should have gone so far, and carried with them the belief that he was an impostor and a robber—a belief which might remain uncontradicted to his dying day—was almost more than he could bear.

From Charles Dickens's *Oliver Twist*

What's on the other side of your mirror?

Alice lifted up her head in some alarm. There was no one to be seen, and her first thought was that she must have been dreaming about the Lion and the Unicorn and those queer Anglo-Saxon Messengers. However, there was the great dish still lying at her feet, on which she had tried to cut the plum-cake, "So I wasn't dreaming, after all," she said to herself, "unless—unless we're all part of the same dream. Only I do hope it's MY dream, and not the Red King's! I don't like belonging to another person's dream," she went on in a rather complaining tone: "I've a great mind to go and wake him, and see what happens!"

From Lewis Carroll's *Through the Looking-Glass*

What is your favorite urban legend?

The road that led to it, and the bridge itself, were thickly shaded by overhanging trees, which cast a gloom about it, even in the daytime; but occasioned a fearful darkness at night. Such was one of the favorite haunts of the Headless Horseman, and the place where he was most frequently encountered. The tale was told of old Brouwer, a most heretical disbeliever in ghosts, how he met the Horseman returning from his foray into Sleepy Hollow, and was obliged to get up behind him; how they galloped over bush and brake, over hill and swamp, until they reached the bridge; when the Horseman suddenly turned into a skeleton, threw old Brouwer into the brook, and sprang away over the tree-tops with a clap of thunder.

From Washington Irving's *The Legend of Sleepy Hollow*

What did you dream about last night?

O, I am out of breath in this fond chase!
The more my prayer, the lesser is my grace.
Happy is Hermia, wheresoe'er she lies,
For she hath blessed and attractive eyes.
How came her eyes so bright? Not with salt
    tears;
If so, my eyes are oft'ner wash'd than hers.
No, no, I am as ugly as a bear,
For beasts that meet me run away for fear;
Therefore no marvel though Demetrius
Do, as a monster, fly my presence thus.
What wicked and dissembling glass of mine
Made me compare with Hermia's sphery eyne?
But who is here? Lysander! on the ground!
Dead, or asleep? I see no blood, no wound.
Lysander, if you live, good sir, awake.

From William Shakespeare's *A Midsummer-Night's Dream*

Where would you travel back in time to?

The tiled floor was thick with dust, and a remarkable array of miscellaneous objects was shrouded in the same grey covering. Then I perceived, standing strange and gaunt in the centre of the hall, what was clearly the lower part of a huge skeleton. I recognized by the oblique feet that it was some extinct creature after the fashion of the Megatherium. The skull and the upper bones lay beside it in the thick dust, and in one place, where rain-water had dropped through a leak in the roof, the thing itself had been worn away. Further in the gallery was the huge skeleton barrel of a Brontosaurus. My museum hypothesis was confirmed.

From H.G. Wells's *The Time Machine*

What do you keep hidden away from others?

He lifted the hangings from the wall, uncovering the second door: this, too, he opened. In a room without a window, there burnt a fire guarded by a high and strong fender, and a lamp suspended from the ceiling by a chain. Grace Poole bent over the fire, apparently cooking something in a saucepan. In the deep shade, at the farther end of the room, a figure ran backwards and forwards. What it was, whether beast or human being, one could not, at first sight, tell: it grovelled, seemingly, on all fours; it snatched and growled like some strange wild animal: but it was covered with clothing, and a quantity of dark, grizzled hair, wild as a mane, hid its head and face.

From Charlotte Brontë's *Jane Eyre*

What is the craziest adventure you've ever been on?

The other pirates were looking their last, too; and they all looked so long that they came near letting the current drift them out of the range of the island. But they discovered the danger in time, and made shift to avert it. About two o'clock in the morning the raft grounded on the bar two hundred yards above the head of the island, and they waded back and forth until they had landed their freight. Part of the little raft's belongings consisted of an old sail, and this they spread over a nook in the bushes for a tent to shelter their provisions; but they themselves would sleep in the open air in good weather, as became outlaws.

From Mark Twain's *The Adventures of Tom Sawyer*

If you were given a major loan, what would you use it on?

The tiresome old person can stay where he is, as far as I am concerned; I don't care about him or his will either, for I am free from care now. (Jumps up.) My goodness, it's delightful to think of, Christine! Free from care! To be able to be free from care, quite free from care; to be able to play and romp with the children; to be able to keep the house beautifully and have everything just as Torvald likes it! And, think of it, soon the spring will come and the big blue sky! Perhaps we shall be able to take a little trip--perhaps I shall see the sea again! Oh, it's a wonderful thing to be alive and be happy.

From Henrik Ibsen's *A Doll's House*

Describe an average day at your job.

Conceive a man by nature and misfortune prone to a pallid hopelessness, can any business seem more fitted to heighten it than that of continually handling these dead letters, and assorting them for the flames? For by the cart-load they are annually burned. Sometimes from out the folded paper the pale clerk takes a ring:—the finger it was meant for, perhaps, moulders in the grave; a bank-note sent in swiftest charity:—he whom it would relieve, nor eats nor hungers any more; pardon for those who died despairing; hope for those who died unhoping; good tidings for those who died stifled by unrelieved calamities. On errands of life, these letters speed to death.

From Herman Melville's "Bartleby, the Scrivener"

CHAPTER SEVEN

A Little Faux Wisdom

What's the best part of getting Chinese takeout? The fortune cookie, of course! In this chapter, you'll get to try your hand at creating some of your very own, so get ready to summon your inner Confucius. You'll have to use the words in the following passages to form a profound statement worthy of a cookie. If you're having trouble coming up with some sage advice, look to our blackout example for guidance.

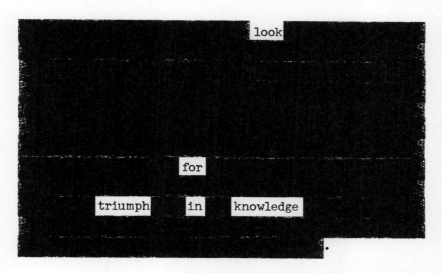

From Charles Dickens's *Great Expectations*

Message: look for triumph in knowledge.

She hoped for a son; he would be strong and dark; she would call him George; and this idea of having a male child was like an expected revenge for all her impotence in the past. A man, at least, is free; he may travel over passions and over countries, overcome obstacles, taste of the most far-away pleasures. But a woman is always hampered. At once inert and flexible, she has against her the weakness of the flesh and legal dependence. Her will, like the veil of her bonnet, held by a string, flutters in every wind; there is always some desire that draws her, some conventionality that restrains.

From Gustave Flaubert's *Madame Bovary*

I went to the woods because I wished to live deliberately, to front only the essential facts of life, and see if I could not learn what it had to teach, and not, when I came to die, discover that I had not lived. I did not wish to live what was not life, living is so dear; nor did I wish to practise resignation, unless it was quite necessary. I wanted to live deep and suck out all the marrow of life, to live so sturdily and Spartan-like as to put to rout all that was not life, to cut a broad swath and shave close, to drive life into a corner, and reduce it to its lowest terms.

From Henry David Thoreau's *Walden; or, Life in the Woods*

She shouts like one possessed into mine ear,
'These are your doings, this your work, I trow.
You stole Orestes from my gripe, and placed
His life with fosterers; but you shall pay
Full penalty.' So harsh is her exclaim.
And he at hand, the husband she extols,
Hounds on the cry, that prince of cowardice,
From head to foot one mass of pestilent harm.
Tongue-doughty champion of this women's-
    war.
I, for Orestes ever languishing
To end this, am undone. For evermore
Intending, still delaying, he wears out
All hope, both here and yonder. How, then,
    friends,
Can I be moderate, or feel the touch
Of holy resignation? Evil fruit
Cannot but follow on a life of ill.

From Sophocles's *Electra*

The cause of America is in a great measure the cause of all mankind. Many circumstances hath, and will arise, which are not local, but universal, and through which the principles of all Lovers of Mankind are affected, and in the Event of which, their Affections are interested. The laying a Country desolate with Fire and Sword, declaring War against the natural rights of all Mankind, and extirpating the Defenders thereof from the Face of the Earth, is the Concern of every Man to whom Nature hath given the Power of feeling; of which Class, regardless of Party Censure, is the AUTHOR.

From Thomas Paine's *Common Sense*

In truth, all through the haunted forest there could be nothing more frightful than the figure of Goodman Brown. On he flew among the black pines, brandishing his staff with frenzied gestures, now giving vent to an inspiration of horrid blasphemy, and now shouting forth such laughter as set all the echoes of the forest laughing like demons around him. The fiend in his own shape is less hideous than when he rages in the breast of man. Thus sped the demoniac on his course, until, quivering among the trees, he saw a red light before him, as when the felled trunks and branches of a clearing have been set on fire, and throw up their lurid blaze against the sky, at the hour of midnight.

From Nathaniel Hawthorne's "Young Goodman Brown"

Lo, Dan Solomon! the wise king; I trow he had more wives than one, as would God I had leave to be refreshed half so oft as he! What a gift of God he had in all his wives! God be praised that I have wedded five, from whom I have plucked their best. Diverse schools make perfect clerks; diverse practice, in many sundry labours, maketh the workman thoroughly perfect; of five husbands am I the scholar. Welcome the sixth, whensoever he shall come. In sooth, I will not for aye keep me chaste. When mine husband is departed from the world, some Christian man shall wed me anon; for then, the apostle saith, I am free to wed, in God's name, where I list.

From Geoffrey Chaucer's *The Canterbury Tales*

Just as in a clock, the result of the complicated motion of innumerable wheels and pulleys is merely a slow and regular movement of the hands which show the time, so the result of all the complicated human activities of 160,000 Russians and French—all their passions, desires, remorse, humiliations, sufferings, outbursts of pride, fear, and enthusiasm—was only the loss of the battle of Austerlitz, the so-called battle of the three Emperors—that is to say, a slow movement of the hand on the dial of human history.

From Leo Tolstoy's *War and Peace*

All the other animals in the forest naturally expect me to be brave, for the Lion is everywhere thought to be the King of Beasts. I learned that if I roared very loudly every living thing was frightened and got out of my way. Whenever I've met a man I've been awfully scared; but I just roared at him, and he has always run away as fast as he could go. If the elephants and the tigers and the bears had ever tried to fight me, I should have run myself—I'm such a coward; but just as soon as they hear me roar they all try to get away from me, and of course I let them go.

From L. Frank Baum's *The Wonderful Wizard of Oz*

When Cosette went out with him, she leaned on his arm, proud and happy, in the plenitude of her heart. Jean Valjean felt his heart melt within him with delight, at all these sparks of a tenderness so exclusive, so wholly satisfied with himself alone. The poor man trembled, inundated with angelic joy; he declared to himself ecstatically that this would last all their lives; he told himself that he really had not suffered sufficiently to merit so radiant a bliss, and he thanked God, in the depths of his soul, for having permitted him to be loved thus, he, a wretch, by that innocent being.

From Victor Hugo's *Les Misérables*

CHAPTER EIGHT

On the Contrary

You'll find out if opposites really attract in this challenging chapter. In order to solve the following puzzles, you'll have to create a contrasting message from the content we've provided. That means that if a passage revolves around a sappy romance between two characters, you'll have to make them fall out of love and quickly. Some puzzles will be harder than others, so if you get stumped, just make sure the theme of each message is completely different from the story as seen in the example we've given.

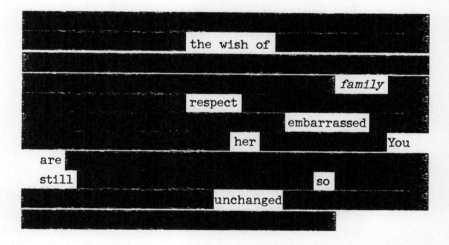

From Jane Austen's *Pride and Prejudice*

Message: the wish of *family* respect embarrassed her/ You are still so unchanged

Oh! But he was a tight-fisted hand at the grindstone, Scrooge! a squeezing, wrenching, grasping, scraping, clutching, covetous, old sinner! Hard and sharp as flint, from which no steel had ever struck out generous fire; secret, and self-contained, and solitary as an oyster. The cold within him froze his old features, nipped his pointed nose, shrivelled his cheek, stiffened his gait; made his eyes red, his thin lips blue; and spoke out shrewdly in his grating voice. A frosty rime was on his head, and on his eyebrows, and his wiry chin. He carried his own low temperature always about with him; he iced his office in the dog-days; and didn't thaw it one degree at Christmas.

From Charles Dickens's *A Christmas Carol*

Here was a population, low-class and mostly foreign, hanging always on the verge of starvation, and dependent for its opportunities of life upon the whim of men every bit as brutal and unscrupulous as the old-time slave drivers; under such circumstances immorality was exactly as inevitable, and as prevalent, as it was under the system of chattel slavery. Things that were quite unspeakable went on there in the packing houses all the time, and were taken for granted by everybody; only they did not show, as in the old slavery times, because there was no difference in color between master and slave.

From Upton Sinclair's *The Jungle*

After all those warlike attempts, the vast confusions, and the consumption both of treasure and of people that must follow them, perhaps upon some misfortune they might be forced to throw up all at last; therefore it seemed much more eligible that the king should improve his ancient kingdom all he could, and make it flourish as much as possible; that he should love his people, and be beloved of them; that he should live among them, govern them gently and let other kingdoms alone, since that which had fallen to his share was big enough, if not too big, for him.

From Thomas More's *Utopia*

Heard melodies are sweet, but those unheard Are sweeter; therefore, ye soft pipes, play on; Not to the sensual ear, but, more endear'd, Pipe to the spirit ditties of no tone: Fair youth, beneath the trees, thou canst not leave Thy song, nor ever can those trees be bare; Bold Lover, never, never canst thou kiss, Though winning near the goal—yet, do not grieve; She cannot fade, though thou hast not thy bliss, For ever wilt thou love, and she be fair! Ah, happy, happy boughs! that cannot shed Your leaves, nor ever bid the Spring adieu; And, happy melodist, unwearied, For ever piping songs for ever new; More happy love! more happy, happy love!

From John Keats's "Ode to a Grecian Urn"

Let me see her face
Again. Why didst thou not pity her? What
An excellent honest man mightst thou have
    been,
If thou hadst borne her to some sanctuary!
Or, bold in a good cause, oppos'd thyself,
With thy advanced sword above thy head,
Between her innocence and my revenge!
I bade thee, when I was distracted of my wits,
Go kill my dearest friend, and thou hast done
    't.
For let me but examine well the cause:
What was the meanness of her match to me?
Only I must confess I had a hope,
Had she continu'd widow, to have gain'd
An infinite mass of treasure by her death:
And that was the main cause,—her marriage,
That drew a stream of gall quite through my
    heart.

From John Webster's *The Duchess of Malfi*

He thought I was asleep first, but I wasn't, and lay there for hours trying to decide whether that front pattern and the back pattern really did move together or separately. On a pattern like this, by daylight, there is a lack of sequence, a defiance of law, that is a constant irritant to a normal mind. The color is hideous enough, and unreliable enough, and infuriating enough, but the pattern is torturing. You think you have mastered it, but just as you get well underway in following, it turns a back-somersault and there you are. It slaps you in the face, knocks you down, and tramples upon you. It is like a bad dream.

From Charlotte Perkins Gilman's "The Yellow Wallpaper"

They were like judges debating over the sentence upon a criminal; they were like ghouls with an immobile corpse in a tomb beside them. I don't think that Leonora was any more to blame than the girl—though Leonora was the more active of the two. Leonora, as I have said, was the perfectly normal woman. I mean to say that in normal circumstances her desires were those of the woman who is needed by society. She desired children, decorum, an establishment; she desired to avoid waste, she desired to keep up appearances. She was utterly and entirely normal even in her utterly undeniable beauty. But I don't mean to say that she acted perfectly normally in this perfectly abnormal situation.

From Ford Madox Ford's *The Good Soldier*

Alack! shall we thus depart indeed?

Our Lady, help, without any more comfort,

Lo, *Fellowship* forsaketh me in my most need:

For help in this world whither shall I resort?

Fellowship herebefore with me would merry
    make;

And now little sorrow for me doth he take.

It is said, in prosperity men friends may find,

Which in adversity be full unkind.

Now whither for succour shall I flee,

Sith that *Fellowship* hath forsaken me?

To my kinsmen I will truly,

Praying them to help me in my necessity;

I believe that they will do so,

For kind will creep where it may not go.

I will go say, for yonder I see them go.

Where be ye now, my friends and kinsmen?

From *Everyman: A Morality Play*

A Syllabic Musing

This chapter is sure to cause a ruckus! To complete these lively puzzles, you'll have to create a message using two filler words (prepositions and/or articles only!) and words with a certain number of syllables. Sure, you'll probably be able to handle one-syllabled words, but what about two- or three-syllabled words? You may find it helpful to reference the message we've created, or sound out the words if you're having a hard time figuring out the number of syllables in each word.

Create a message using two-syllabled words.

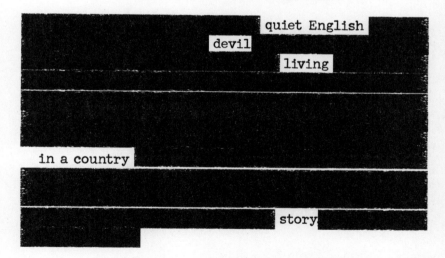

From Wilkie Collins's *The Moonstone*

Message: quiet English devil living in a country story

Create a message using one-syllabled words.

Emma's eyes were instantly withdrawn; and she sat silently meditating, in a fixed attitude, for a few minutes. A few minutes were sufficient for making her acquainted with her own heart. A mind like hers, once opening to suspicion, made rapid progress. She touched—she admitted—she acknowledged the whole truth. Why was it so much worse that Harriet should be in love with Mr. Knightley, than with Frank Churchill? Why was the evil so dreadfully increased by Harriet's having some hope of a return? It darted through her, with the speed of an arrow, that Mr. Knightley must marry no one but herself!

From Jane Austen's *Emma*

Create a message using one-syllabled words.

I like her with all her faults; nay, like her for her faults. Her follies are so natural, or so artful, that they become her, and those affectations which in another woman would be odious serve but to make her more agreeable. I'll tell thee, Fainall, she once used me with that insolence that in revenge I took her to pieces, sifted her, and separated her failings: I studied 'em and got 'em by rote. The catalogue was so large that I was not without hopes, one day or other, to hate her heartily. To which end I so used myself to think of 'em, that at length, contrary to my design and expectation, they gave me every hour less and less disturbance.

From William Congreve's *The Way of the World*

Create a message using two-syllabled words.

If I do prove her haggard,
Though that her jesses were my dear
   heartstrings,
I'd whistle her off, and let her down the wind
To prey at fortune. Haply, for I am black,
And have not those soft parts of conversation
That chamberers have; or for I am declin'd
Into the vale of years,—yet that's not much,—
She's gone; I am abus'd, and my relief
Must be to loathe her. O curse of marriage,
That we can call these delicate creatures ours,
And not their appetites! I had rather be a toad,
And live upon the vapor of a dungeon,
Than keep a corner in the thing I love
For others' uses. Yet, 'tis the plague of great
   ones:
Prerogativ'd are they less than the base;
'Tis destiny unshunnable, like death

From William Shakespeare's *Othello*

Create a message using three-syllabled words.

Well, to speak with perfect candour, Cecily, I wish that you were fully forty-two, and more than usually plain for your age. Ernest has a strong upright nature. He is the very soul of truth and honour. Disloyalty would be as impossible to him as deception. But even men of the noblest possible moral character are extremely susceptible to the influence of the physical charms of others. Modern, no less than Ancient History, supplies us with many most painful examples of what I refer to. If it were not so, indeed, History would be quite unreadable.

From Oscar Wilde's *The Importance of Being Ernest*

Create a message using two-syllabled words.

There was room for her, after all, in this crowded selfish world of pleasure whence, so short a time since, her poverty had seemed to exclude her. These people whom she had ridiculed and yet envied were glad to make a place for her in the charmed circle about which all her desires revolved. They were not as brutal and self-engrossed as she had fancied—or rather, since it would no longer be necessary to flatter and humour them, that side of their nature became less conspicuous. Society is a revolving body which is apt to be judged according to its place in each man's heaven; and at present it was turning its illuminated face to Lily.

From Edith Wharton's *The House of Mirth*

Create a message using one-syllabled words.

I wonder, for it is hard for me to conceive how men who knew the word "I," could give it up and not know what they had lost. But such has been the story, for I have lived in the City of the damned, and I know what horror men permitted to be brought upon them. Perhaps, in those days, there were a few among men, a few of clear sight and clean soul, who refused to surrender that word. What agony must have been theirs before that which they saw coming and could not stop! Perhaps they cried out in protest and in warning. But men paid no heed to their warning.

From Ayn Rand's *Anthem*

Create a message using two-syllabled words.

Above all, don't lie to yourself. The man who lies to himself and listens to his own lie comes to such a pass that he cannot distinguish the truth within him, or around him, and so loses all respect for himself and for others. And having no respect he ceases to love, and in order to occupy and distract himself without love he gives way to passions and coarse pleasures, and sinks to bestiality in his vices, all from continual lying to other men and to himself. The man who lies to himself can be more easily offended than any one.

From Fyodor Dostoyevsky's *The Brothers Karamazov*

163

Create a message using three-syllabled words.

Out of the window perilously spread
Her drying combinations touched by the sun's
   last rays,
On the divan are piled (at night her bed)
Stockings, slippers, camisoles, and stays.
I Tiresias, old man with wrinkled dugs
Perceived the scene, and foretold the rest -
I too awaited the expected guest.
He, the young man carbuncular, arrives,
A small house agent's clerk, with one bold
   stare,
One of the low on whom assurance sits
As a silk hat on a Bradford millionaire.
The time is now propitious, as he guesses,
The meal is ended, she is bored and tired,
Endeavours to engage her in caresses
Which still are unreproved, if undesired.
Flushed and decided, he assaults at once;
Exploring hands encounter no defence.

From T.S. Eliot's *The Waste Land*

CHAPTER TEN

One for the Books

The challenge in this chapter isn't in creating a message, but picking the *right* words. You can only use one word per line to complete each puzzle, but you can skip a line if you get stuck. And don't even think about cheating on this one—you can only use ink!

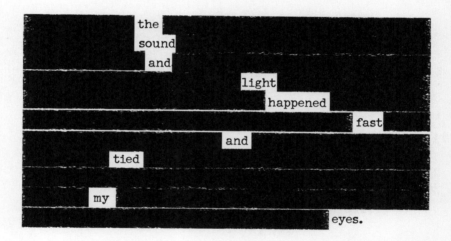

From Jonathan Swift's *Gulliver's Travels into Several Remote Regions of the World*

Message: the sound and light happened fast and tied my eyes.

In the first place, his startling likeness to Catherine connected him fearfully with her. That, however, which you may suppose the most potent to arrest my imagination, is actually the least: for what is not connected with her to me? and what does not recall her? I cannot look down to this floor, but her features are shaped in the flags! In every cloud, in every tree—filling the air at night, and caught by glimpses in every object by day—I am surrounded with her image! The most ordinary faces of men and women—my own features—mock me with a resemblance. The entire world is a dreadful collection of memoranda that she did exist, and that I have lost her!

From Emily Brontë's *Wuthering Heights*

It seemed to her that she had been in the timber trade for ages and ages, and that the most important and necessary thing in life was timber; and there was something intimate and touching to her in the very sound of words such as "baulk," "post," "beam," "pole," "scantling," "batten," "lath," "plank," etc. At night when she was asleep she dreamed of perfect mountains of planks and boards, and long strings of wagons, carting timber somewhere far away. She dreamed that a whole regiment of six-inch beams forty feet high, standing on end, was marching upon the timber-yard; that logs, beams, and boards knocked together with the resounding crash of dry wood, kept falling and getting up again, piling themselves on each other.

From Anton Pavlovich Chekhov's "The Darling"

My heart aches, and a drowsy numbness pains
My sense, as though of hemlock I had drunk,
Or emptied some dull opiate to the drains
One minute past, and Lethe-wards had sunk:
'Tis not through envy of thy happy lot,
But being too happy in thine happiness,—
That thou, light-winged Dryad of the trees,
In some melodious plot
Of beechen green, and shadows numberless,
Singest of summer in full-throated ease.
O, for a draught of vintage! that hath been
Cool'd a long age in the deep-delved earth,
Tasting of Flora and the country green,
Dance, and Provençal song, and sunburnt
   mirth!
O for a beaker full of the warm South,
Full of the true, the blushful Hippocrene,
With beaded bubbles winking at the brim.

From John Keats's "Ode to a Nightingale"

A certain light was beginning to dawn dimly within her,—the light which, showing the way, forbids it. At that early period it served but to bewilder her. It moved her to dreams, to thoughtfulness, to the shadowy anguish which had overcome her the midnight when she had abandoned herself to tears. In short, Mrs. Pontellier was beginning to realize her position in the universe as a human being, and to recognize her relations as an individual to the world within and about her. This may seem like a ponderous weight of wisdom to descend upon the soul of a young woman of twenty-eight—perhaps more wisdom than the Holy Ghost is usually pleased to vouchsafe to any woman.

From Kate Chopin's *The Awakening*

I put down my cup and examine my own mind. It is for it to discover the truth. But how? What an abyss of uncertainty whenever the mind feels that some part of it has strayed beyond its own borders; when it, the seeker, is at once the dark region through which it must go seeking, where all its equipment will avail it nothing. Seek? More than that: create. It is face to face with something which does not so far exist, to which it alone can give reality and substance, which it alone can bring into the light of day. And I begin again to ask myself what it could have been...

From Marcel Proust's *Swann's Way*

So peremptorily did these shades beckon him, that each day mankind and the claims of mankind slipped farther from him. Deep in the forest a call was sounding, and as often as he heard this call, mysteriously thrilling and luring, he felt compelled to turn his back upon the fire and the beaten earth around it, and to plunge into the forest, and on and on, he knew not where or why; nor did he wonder where or why, the call sounding imperiously, deep in the forest. But as often as he gained the soft unbroken earth and the green shade, the love for John Thornton drew him back to the fire again.

From Jack London's *The Call of the Wild*

Surely I have my thoughts, and not a few
Have held me strange. To me it seemeth, when
A crafty tongue is given to evil men
'Tis like to wreck, not help them. Their own
   brain
Tempts them with lies to dare and dare again,
Till . . . no man hath enough of subtlety.
As thou—be not so seeming-fair to me
Nor deft of speech. One word will make thee
   fall.
Wert thou not false, 'twas thine to tell me
   all,
And charge me help thy marriage path, as I
Did love thee; not befool me with a lie.

From Euripides's *Medea*

So speaking, she undid the clasp that fastened the scarlet letter, and, taking it from her bosom, threw it to a distance among the withered leaves. The mystic token alighted on the hither verge of the stream. With a hand's-breadth further flight, it would have fallen into the water, and have given the little brook another woe to carry onward, besides the unintelligible tale which it still kept murmuring about. But there lay the embroidered letter, glittering like a lost jewel, which some ill-fated wanderer might pick up, and thenceforth be haunted by strange phantoms of guilt, sinkings of the heart, and unaccountable misfortune.

From Nathaniel Hawthorne's *The Scarlet Letter*

Though he was impatient to see her, he hardly knew what he should say to her about his aunt's refusal to become acquainted with her; but he discovered, promptly enough, that with Miss Daisy Miller there was no great need of walking on tiptoe. He found her that evening in the garden, wandering about in the warm starlight like an indolent sylph, and swinging to and fro the largest fan he had ever beheld. It was ten o'clock. He had dined with his aunt, had been sitting with her since dinner, and had just taken leave of her till the morrow. Miss Daisy Miller seemed very glad to see him; she declared it was the longest evening she had ever passed.

From Henry James's *Daisy Miller*

CHAPTER ELEVEN

Alternating Tidings

Like the previous chapter, you'll have to find the perfect words to complete these puzzles, but this time we made sure to kick it up a notch. Unlike before, you'll only be able to use one word from *every other* line to create a message, which means you'll have to pay extra attention to what you black out. While choosing words line by line is definitely much more exciting, feel free to plan ahead if you'd like.

From William Shakespeare's *A Midsummer-Night's Dream*

Message: no look of Love in Hermia's heat

But the Green Knight began
A low melodious laugh, like running brooks
Whose pebbly babble fills the shadowy nooks
Of green-aisled woodlands, when the winds are still.
"My friend, we bear each other no ill will.
When first I swung my axe, you showed some fear;
I owed you that much for your blow last year.
The second time I swung,—yet spared your life,—
That paid you for the kiss you gave my wife!"
"Your wife!" "My wife, Sir Gawayne; 't was my word;
And when I swung my weapon for the third
And last time, then I made the red blood spirt
For that green girdle underneath your shirt!
You played me false, my friend!"

From *Gawayne and the Green Knight*

Miss Rebecca was not, then, in the least kind or placable. All the world used her ill, said this young misanthropist, and we may be pretty certain that persons whom all the world treats ill, deserve entirely the treatment they get. The world is a looking-glass, and gives back to every man the reflection of his own face. Frown at it, and it will in turn look sourly upon you; laugh at it and with it, and it is a jolly kind companion; and so let all young persons take their choice. This is certain, that if the world neglected Miss Sharp, she never was known to have done a good action in behalf of anybody.

From William Makepeace Thackeray's *Vanity Fair*

His eyes rested on a large photograph of May Welland, which the young girl had given him in the first days of their romance, and which had now displaced all the other portraits on the table. With a new sense of awe he looked at the frank forehead, serious eyes and gay innocent mouth of the young creature whose soul's custodian he was to be. That terrifying product of the social system he belonged to and believed in, the young girl who knew nothing and expected everything, looked back at him like a stranger through May Welland's familiar features; and once more it was borne in on him that marriage was not the safe anchorage he had been taught to think, but a voyage on uncharted seas.

From Edith Wharton's *The Age of Innocence*

While he is drinking, being attracted with the reflection of his own form, seen *in the water*, he falls in love with a thing that has no substance; *and* he thinks that to be a body, which is *but* a shadow. He is astonished at himself, and remains unmoved with the same countenance, like a statue formed of Parian marble. Lying on the ground, he gazes on his eyes *like* two stars, and fingers worthy of Bacchus, and hair worthy of Apollo, and his youthful cheeks and ivory neck, and the comeliness of his mouth, and his blushing complexion mingled with the whiteness of snow; and everything he admires, for which he himself is worthy to be admired. In his ignorance, he covets himself; and he that approves, is himself *the thing* approved.

From Ovid's *Metamorphoses*

Oh, I've dozens of plans, Marilla. I've been thinking them out for a week. I shall give life here my best, and I believe it will give its best to me in return. When I left Queen's my future seemed to stretch out before me like a straight road. I thought I could see along it for many a milestone. Now there is a bend in it. I don't know what lies around the bend, but I'm going to believe that the best does. It has a fascination of its own, that bend, Marilla. I wonder how the road beyond it goes—what there is of green glory and soft, checkered light and shadows—what new landscapes—what new beauties—what curves and hills and valleys further on.

From Lucy Maud Montgomery's *Anne of Green Gables*

A lion, not a man, who slaughters wide,

In strength of rage, and impotence of pride;

Who hastes to murder with a savage joy,

Invades around, and breathes but to destroy!

Shame is not of his soul; nor understood,

The greatest evil and the greatest good.

Still for one loss he rages unresign'd,

Repugnant to the lot of all mankind;

To lose a friend, a brother, or a son,

Heaven dooms each mortal, and its will is done:

Awhile they sorrow, then dismiss their care;

Fate gives the wound, and man is born to bear.

But this insatiate, the commission given

By fate exceeds, and tempts the wrath of heaven:

Lo, how his rage dishonest drags along

Hector's dead earth, insensible of wrong!

From Homer's *The Iliad*

He was not completely unconscious, however, all the time he was ill; he was in a feverish state, sometimes delirious, sometimes half conscious. He remembered a great deal afterwards. Sometimes it seemed as though there were a number of people round him; they wanted to take him away somewhere, there was a great deal of squabbling and discussing about him. Then he would be alone in the room; they had all gone away afraid of him, and only now and then opened the door a crack to look at him; they threatened him, plotted something together, laughed, and mocked at him.

From Fyodor Dostoyevsky's *Crime and Punishment*

The thin grasses, more or less coating the hill, were touched by the wind in breezes of differing powers, and almost of differing natures—one rubbing the blades heavily, another raking them piercingly, another brushing them like a soft broom. The instinctive act of humankind was to stand and listen, and learn how the trees on the right and the trees on the left wailed or chaunted to each other in the regular antiphonies of a cathedral choir; how hedges and other shapes to leeward then caught the note, lowering it to the tenderest sob; and how the hurrying gust then plunged into the south, to be heard no more.

From Thomas Hardy's *Far from the Madding Crowd*

SOMETHING there is that doesn't love a wall,
That sends the frozen-ground-swell under it,
And spills the upper boulders in the sun;
And makes gaps even two can pass abreast.
The work of hunters is another thing:
I have come after them and made repair
Where they have left not one stone on a stone,
But they would have the rabbit out of hiding,
To please the yelping dogs. The gaps I mean,
No one has seen them made or heard them made,
But at spring mending-time we find them there.
I let my neighbour know beyond the hill;
And on a day we meet to walk the line
And set the wall between us once again.

From Robert Frost's "Mending Wall"

CHAPTER TWELVE

More than Symbols

By now you may feel like you've mastered these addicting puzzles, but you haven't seen anything yet! In this final chapter, you'll need to not only create a message, but also construct it in the shape of an object. Sure, our blackout sample may make this chapter look like a piece of cake, but once you get started, you'll definitely see that this challenge is easier said than done. Just remember that you don't have to stick to a certain area of the page, anywhere and any size will do as long as you develop your message in shape. Once you've finished, you'll have a blackout masterpiece truly worth showing of, so make sure you pass it along to friends!

Create a message in the shape of Excalibur.

and in full armour rode out alone to
the knight of the fountain. It was a strong battle
Arthur's spear was all shattered,

From Sir Thomas Malory's *Stories of King Arthur and His Knights*

Message: and in full armour rode out alone the knight of the fountain./ It was a strong battle/ Arthur's spear was all shattered

Create a message in the shape of a skull.

To be, or not to be,—that is the question:—
Whether 'tis nobler in the mind to suffer
The slings and arrows of outrageous fortune
Or to take arms against a sea of troubles,
And by opposing end them?—To die,—to
    sleep,—
No more; and by a sleep to say we end
The heartache, and the thousand natural
    shocks
That flesh is heir to,—'tis a consummation
Devoutly to be wish'd. To die,—to sleep;—
To sleep! perchance to dream:—ay, there's the
    rub;
For in that sleep of death what dreams may
    come,
When we have shuffled off this mortal coil,
Must give us pause: there's the respect
That makes calamity of so long life.

From William Shakespeare's *The Tragedie of Hamlet, Prince of Denmarke*

Create a message in the shape of a triangle.

It was all madness; he was in love, thoroughly attached to Lucy, and engaged,—engaged as strongly as an honorable man need be. He wished he had never seen this Maggie Tulliver, to be thrown into a fever by her in this way; she would make a sweet, strange, troublesome, adorable wife to some man or other, but he would never have chosen her himself. Did she feel as he did? He hoped she did—not. He ought not to have gone. He would master himself in future. He would make himself disagreeable to her, quarrel with her perhaps. Quarrel with her? Was it possible to quarrel with a creature who had such eyes,—defying and deprecating, contradicting and clinging, imperious and beseeching,—full of delicious opposites?

From George Eliot's *The Mill on the Floss*

Create a message in the shape of a bridge.

As he pushes open the gate and passes up the wide white walk, he sees a flutter of female garments; his wife, looking fresh and cool and sweet, steps down from the veranda to meet him. At the bottom of the steps she stands waiting, with a smile of ineffable joy, an attitude of matchless grace and dignity. Ah, how beautiful she is! He springs forwards with extended arms. As he is about to clasp her he feels a stunning blow upon the back of the neck; a blinding white light blazes all about him with a sound like the shock of a cannon— then all is darkness and silence!

From Ambrose Bierce's "An Occurrence at Owl Creek Bridge"

Create a message in the shape of a flower.

There was a laurel-hedged walk which curved round the secret garden and ended at a gate which opened into a wood, in the park. She thought she would slip round this walk and look into the wood and see if there were any rabbits hopping about. She enjoyed the skipping very much and when she reached the little gate she opened it and went through because she heard a low, peculiar whistling sound and wanted to find out what it was. It was a very strange thing indeed. She quite caught her breath as she stopped to look at it. A boy was sitting under a tree, with his back against it, playing on a rough wooden pipe.

From Frances Hodgson Burnett's *The Secret Garden*

Create a message in the shape of a coin.

"Yes, Pip, dear boy, I've made a gentleman on you! It's me wot has done it! I swore that time, sure as ever I earned a guinea, that guinea should go to you. I swore arterwards, sure as ever I spec'lated and got rich, you should get rich. I lived rough, that you should live smooth; I worked hard, that you should be above work. What odds, dear boy? Do I tell it, fur you to feel a obligation? Not a bit. I tell it, fur you to know as that there hunted dunghill dog wot you kep life in, got his head so high that he could make a gentleman,—and, Pip, you're him!"

From Charles Dickens's *Great Expectations*

Create a message in the shape of a blade of grass.

What do you think has become of the young and
   old men?

And what do you think has become of the women
   and children?

They are alive and well somewhere,

The smallest sprout shows there is really no death,

And if ever there was it led forward life, and
   does not wait at the end to arrest it,

And ceas'd the moment life appear'd.

All goes onward and outward, nothing collapses,

And to die is different from what any one
   supposed, and luckier.

Has any one supposed it lucky to be born?

I hasten to inform him or her it is just as lucky
   to die, and I know it.

From Walt Whitman's "A Song of Myself"

Create a message in the shape of a diamond.

The night of the ball arrived. Madame Loisel was a great success. She was prettier than any other woman present, elegant, graceful, smiling and wild with joy. All the men looked at her, asked her name, sought to be introduced. All the attaches of the Cabinet wished to waltz with her. She was remarked by the minister himself. She danced with rapture, with passion, intoxicated by pleasure, forgetting all in the triumph of her beauty, in the glory of her success, in a sort of cloud of happiness comprised of all this homage, admiration, these awakened desires and of that sense of triumph which is so sweet to woman's heart.

From Guy De Maupassant's "The Diamond Necklace"

221

Create a message in the shape of a cabin.

It was on his grave, my friends, that I resolved, before God, that I would never own another slave, while it was possible to free him; that nobody, through me, should ever run the risk of being parted from home and friends, and dying on a lonely plantation, as he died. So, when you rejoice in your freedom, think that you owe it to that good old soul, and pay it back in kindness to his wife and children. Think of your freedom, every time you see UNCLE TOM'S CABIN; and let it be a memorial to put you all in mind to follow in his steps, and be honest and faithful and Christian as he was.

From Harriet Beecher Stowe's *Uncle Tom's Cabin* or, *Life Among the Lowly*

Create a message in the shape of an apple.

Yet let me not forget what I have gain'd
From thir own mouths; all is not theirs it
   seems:
One fatal Tree there stands of Knowledge
   call'd,
Forbidden them to taste: Knowledge forbidd'n?
Suspicious, reasonless. Why should thir Lord
Envie them that? can it be sin to know,
Can it be death? and do they onely stand
By Ignorance, is that thir happie state,
The proof of thir obedience and thir faith?
O fair foundation laid whereon to build
Thir ruine! Hence I will excite thir minds
With more desire to know, and to reject
Envious commands, invented with designe
To keep them low whom knowledge might exalt
Equal with Gods; aspiring to be such,
They taste and die: what likelier can ensue?

From John Milton's *Paradise Lost*

Create a message in the shape of a boat.

Of course the Neverlands vary a good deal. John's, for instance, had a lagoon with flamingoes flying over it at which John was shooting, while Michael, who was very small, had a flamingo with lagoons flying over it. John lived in a boat turned upside down on the sands, Michael in a wigwam, Wendy in a house of leaves deftly sewn together. John had no friends, Michael had friends at night, Wendy had a pet wolf forsaken by its parents. But on the whole the Neverlands have a family resemblance, and if they stood still in a row you could say of them that they have each other's nose, and so forth. On these magic shores children at play are for ever beaching their coracles. We too have been there; we can still hear the sound of the surf, though we shall land no more.

From J.M. Barrie's *Peter and Wendy*

Create a message in the shape of a circle.

Jack presently brought a very pretty pigeon, unlike the rest, to show me, as he felt unwilling to kill it; and seeing that it must be one of our own European breed, which we wished to preserve until their numbers greatly increased, I took the trembling captive, and gently cleaned its feet and wings with oil and ashes from the stiff, sticky mess with which it was bedaubed, placing it then in a wicker cage, and telling Jack to bring me any others like it which were caught. This he did; and we secured several pairs, greatly to my satisfaction, as having necessarily let them go free when we landed, they had become quite wild, and we derived no advantage from them: whereas now we would have a cot, and pigeon-pie whenever we liked.

From Johann David Wyss's *The Swiss Family Robinson*

Bibliography

Alcott, Louisa May. *Little Women*. Boston: Roberts Brothers, 1869.

Alighieri, Dante. *The Divine Comedy*. Trans. Rev. Henry Francis Cary, MA. London: Cassell and Company, 1892.

Austen, Jane. *Emma*. London: John Murray, 1816.

Austen, Jane. *Pride and Prejudice*. Cambridge: John Wilson and Son, 1892.

Austen, Jane. *Sense and Sensibility*. London: Whitehall, 1811.

Barrie, J.M. *Peter and Wendy*. New York: Charles Scribner's Sons, 1912.

Baum, Frank L. *The Wonderful Wizard of Oz*. New York: G.M. Hill Co., 1900.

Bierce, Ambrose. "An Occurrence at Owl Creek Bridge." *Tales of Soldiers and Civilians*. New York: Lovell, Corvell & Company, 1891.

Brontë, Charlotte. *Jane Eyre*. London: Smith, Elder & Co., 1847.

Brontë, Emily. *Wuthering Heights*. London: Thomas Caultey Newby, 1847.

Burnett, Frances Hodgson. *The Secret Garden*. New York: Frederick A. Stokes Company, 1911.

Carroll, Lewis. *Through the Looking-Glass*. London: Macmillian, 1871.

Chaucer, Geoffrey. *The Canterbury Tales of Geoffrey Chaucer*. Ed. Percy MacKaye. New York: Duffield & Company 1914.

Chekhov, Anton Pavlovich. "The Darling." *The Darling and Other Stories*. Trans. Constance Garrett. London: Chatto and Windus, 1926.

Chekhov, Anton Pavlovich. "Uncle Vanya." Plays by Anton Tchekoff, Trans. Marian Fell. New York: Charles Scribner's Sons, 1916.

Chopin, Kate. *The Awakening*. New York: Herbert S. Stone & Company, 1899.

Christie, Agatha. *The Secret Adversary*. London: The Bodley Head, 1922.

Collins, Wilkie. *The Moonstone*. London: Tinsley Brothers, 1868.

Congreve, William. *The Way of the World*. London: Methuen & Co., 1895.

Conrad, Joseph. *Heart of Darkness*. London: *Blackwood's Magazine*, 1902.

Conrad, Joseph. *Lord Jim*. London: Nelson Doubleday, 1900.

Defoe, Daniel. *The Life and Adventures of Robinson Crusoe*. London: Seeley, Service & Co., 1919.

De Maupassant, Guy. "The Diamond Necklace." *The Works of Guy De Maupassant*. New York: Bigelow, Smith & Co., 1909.

Dickens, Charles. *A Tale of Two Cities*. London: Chapman & Hall, 1859.

Dickens, Charles. *Great Expectations*. London: Chapman & Hall, 1861.

Dickens, Charles. *Oliver Twist*. London: Richard Bentley, 1839.

Dickens, Charles. *A Christmas Carol*. London: Chapman & Hall, 1843.

Doyle, Sir Arthur Conan. *Adventures of Sherlock Holmes*. New York: Harper & Brothers, 1902.

Dostoyevsky, Fyodor. *The Brothers Karamazov*. Trans. Constance Garnett. New York: The Lowell Press, 1879.

Dostoyevsky, Fyodor. *Crime and Punishment*. Trans. Constance Garnett. New York: P. F. Collier & Son, 1917.

Dumas, Alexandre. *The Count of Monte Cristo*. London: Chapman & Hall, 1846.

Eliot, George. *Middlemarch*. London: William Blackwood and Sons, 1871.

Eilot, George. *The Mill on the Floss*. New York: Harper & Brothers, 1860.

Eliot, T.S. *The Waste Land*. New York: Boni and Liveright, 1922.

Euripides. *The Medea of Euripides*. Trans. Gilbert Murray, MA, LLD. New York: Oxford University Press, 1912.

Fielding, Henry. "Tom Jones." *The Miscellaneous Works of Henry Fielding*. New York: H.W. Derby, 1861.

Flaubert, Gustave. *Madame Bovary*. Trans. Eleanor Marx. London: W.W. Gibbings, 1892.

Ford, Ford Madox. *The Good Solider*. London: The Bodley Head, 1915.

Frost, Robert. "Home Burial." *North of Boston*. New York: Henry Holt and Company, 1917.

Frost, Robert. "Mending Wall." *North of Boston*. New York: Henry Holt and Company, 1917.

Gilman, Charlotte Perkins. "The Yellow Wallpaper." *New England Magazine*, 1892.

Hardy, Thomas. *Far from the Madding Crowd*. New York: Harper & Brothers, 1912.

Hardy, Thomas. *Tess of the d'Urbervilles*. New York: Nelson Doubleday, 1891.

Hawthorne, Nathaniel. *The Scarlet Letter*. Boston: Ticknor, Reed, and Fields, 1850.

Hawthorne, Nathaniel. *The House of Seven Gables*. Boston: Ticknor, Reed, and Fields, 1851.

Hawthorne, Nathaniel. "Young Goodman Brown." *Mosses from An Old Manse*. London: Wiley & Putnam, 1846.

Homer. *The Iliad of Homer*. Trans. William Cowper. New York: D. Appleton & Co., 1860.

Hugo, Victor. *The Hunchback of Notre-Dame*. London: Richard Bentley, 1849.

Hugo, Victor. *Les Misérables*. Trans. Isabel F. Hapgood. New York: Thomas Y. Crowell & Co., 1887.

Ibsen, Henrik. "A Doll's House." *A Doll's House: and Two Other Plays*. E.P. Dutton & Co., 1910.

Irving, Washington. "The Legend of Sleepy Hollow." *The Sketch Book of Geoffrey Crayon, Gent*. London: C.S. Van Winkle, 1819.

James, Henry. *The Ambassadors*. New York: Harper & Brothers, 1903.

James, Henry. *Daisy Miller*. London: Harper & Brothers, 1879.

Joyce, James. *A Portrait of an Artist as a Young Man*. New York: B.W. Huebsch, 1916.

Keats, John. "Ode to a Grecian Urn." *Keats Poems Published in 1820*. Ed. M. Robertson. London: The Clarendon Press, 1909.

Keats, John. "Ode to a Nightingale." *Keats Poems Published in 1820*. Ed. M. Robertson. London: The Clarendon Press, 1909.

Lawrence, D.H. *Sons and Lovers*. London: Gerald Duckworth and Company Ltd., 1913.

Lewis, Charlton Miner. *Gawayne and the Green Knight*. New Haven: Yale University Press, 1903.

Lewis, Sinclair. *Babbitt*. New York: Harcourt, Brace & Co., 1922.

London, Jack. *The Call of the Wild*. New York: Macmillian, 1903.

Malory, Sir Thomas. *Stories of King Arthur and His Knights*. London: George G. Harrap & Company, 1905.

Melville, Herman. *Moby-Dick: The Whale*. New York: Harper & Brothers, 1851.

Melville, Herman. "Bartleby, the Scrivener." *The Piazza Tales*. New York: Dix & Edwards, 1856.

Milton, John. *Paradise Lost*. New York: D. Appleton & Co., 1851.

Montgomery, Lucy Maud. *Anne of Green Gables*. Boston: L.C. Page & Co., 1908.

More, Thomas. *Utopia*. Trans. Gilbert Burnet. London: Cassell & Company, 1901.

Moses, Montrose J., Ed. *Everyman: A Morality Play*. New York: K.F. Taylor & Company, 1903.

Ovid. *Metamorphoses*. Trans. Henry T. Riley, MA. New York: George Hill & Sons, 1893.

Paine, Thomas. "Common Sense." *The Writings of Thomas Paine*. Ed. Moncure Daniel Conway. New York: G.P. Putnam's Sons, 1894.

Poe, Edgar Allan. "The Fall of the House of Usher." *Tales of the Grotesque and Arabesque*. Philadelphia: Lea and Blanchard, 1840.

Proust, Marcel. *Swann's Way*. Trans. C. K. Scott Moncrieff. New York: Henry Holt and Company, 1922.

Rand, Ayn. *Anthem*. London: Cassell & Company, 1938.

Shakespeare, William. *A Midsummer-Night's Dream*. Ed. Brainerd Kellogg, AM. New York: Maynard, Merrill, & Co., 1890.

Shakespeare, William. *The Tragedie of Hamlet, Prince of Denmarke*. Ed. George MacDonald. London: Longmans, Green, and Co., 1885.

Shakespeare, William. *The Tragedie of Macbeth*. Ed. Mark Harvey Liddell. New York: Doubleday, Page & Co., 1903.

Shakespeare, William. *The Tragedy of Othello*. Ed. H.C. Hart. London: Meuthen and Co., 1903.

Shaw, George Bernard. *Pygmalion*. New York: Brentano, 1916.

Shelley, Percy Bysshe. "To a Skylark." *Prometheus Unbound A Lyrical Drama in Four Acts With Other Poems*. London: C. and J. Ollier, 1828.

Sinclair, Upton. *The Jungle*. New York: Nelson Doubleday, 1906.

Sophocles. "Antigone." *The Tragedies of Sophocles*. Trans. Richard C. Jebb. Cambridge: Cambridge University Press, 1904.

Sophocles. "Electra." *The Tragedies of Sophocles*. Trans. Richard C. Jebb. Cambridge: Cambridge University Press, 1904.

Sophocles. "Opedius the King." *The Tragedies of Sophocles*. Trans. Richard C. Jebb. Cambridge: Cambridge University Press, 1904.

Spenser, Edmund. *Spenser's The Faerie Queene*. Ed. George Armstrng Wauchope, MA, PHD. New York: The MacMillan Company, 1921.

Stowe, Harriet Beecher. *Uncle Tom's Cabin or, Life Among the Lowly*. Boston: Houghton, Mifflin, and Company, 1899.

Swift, Jonathan. *Gulliver's Travels Into Several Remote Regions of the World*. Boston: D.C. Heath & Co., Publishers, 1900.

Thackeray, William Makepeace. *Vanity Fair*. London: Bradbury and Evans, 1849.

Thoreau, Henry David. *Walden; or, Life in the Woods*. Boston: Ticknor and Fields, 1854.

Tolstoy, Leo. *Anna Karenin*. Trans. Constance Garrett. New York: P.F. Collier & Son, 1917.

Tolstoy, Leo. *War and Peace*. London: J.M. Dent & Co., 1904.

Trollope, Anthony. *Can You Forgive Her?* London: Chapman & Hall, 1865.

Twain, Mark. *The Adventures of Huckleberry Finn*. New York: Charles L. Webster and Company, 1885.

Twain, Mark. *The Adventures of Tom Sawyer*. Hartford: American, 1884.

Virgil. *Aeneid*. Trans. John Dryden. New York: P.F. Collier & Son, 1909.

Voltaire. *Candide*. New York: Boni & Liveright, Inc., 1918.

Webster, John. *The Duchess of Malfi*. Ed. C. Waughan, MA. London: J.M. Dent and Co., 1900.

Wells, H.G. *The Time Machine*. London: William Heinemann, 1895.

Wharton, Edith. *The Age of Innocence*. New York: D. Appleton and Company, 1920.

Wharton, Edith. The *House of Mirth*. New York: *Charles Scribner's Sons, 1905*.

Whitman, Walt. "Song of Myself." *Leaves of Grass*. Boston: Small, Maynard & Company, 1897.

Wilde, Oscar. *The Importance of Being Ernest*. London: Meuthen & Co. Ltd., 1899.

Wilde, Oscar. *The Picture of Dorian Gray*. London: Ward, Lock, and Company, 1891.

Wyatt, Alfred John, Ed. *Beowulf*. Cambridge: Cambridge University Press, 1894.

Wyss, Johann David. *The Swiss Family Robinson*. New York: Macmillian & Co. Limited, 1907.